# I Want to Know · About JESUS

# Rick Osborne and K. Christie Bowler

## ZondervanPublishingHouse
*Grand Rapids, Michigan*

*A Division of HarperCollins Publishers*

**21**

**For Lightwave**
   Managing Editor: Elaine Osborne
   Art Director: Terry Van Roon

*Jesus* copyright © 1998 by The Zondervan Corporation.

Artwork and Text copyright © 1998 by Lightwave
   Publishing Inc. All rights reserved.
   http://www.lightwavepublishing.com

Scripture portions taken from the *Holy Bible, New International
   Reader's Version* Copyright © 1994,
   1996 by International Bible Society.

Photo on page 23 courtesy of Zondervan Publishing House.

**Library of Congress Cataloging-in-Publication Data**

Osborne, Rick, 1961–      .
         Jesus / Rick Osborne.
              p.   cm.—(I want to know™)
         Summary: Relates the major stories in the life of Jesus,
   including his birth, miracles, teachings, death, and resurrection, and explores who he was and what his mission was.
         ISBN 0–310–22087–4 (hardcover)
         1.   Jesus Christ—Juvenile literature.
   [1. Jesus Christ.]   I. Title. II. Series: Osborne, Rick, 1961–
   . I want to know™.
   BT302.077    1998
   232—dc21                                97-38953
                                           CIP
                                           AC

This edition is printed on acid-free paper and meets the American
   National Standards Institute Z39.48 standard.

Published by Zondervan Publishing House, Grand Rapids,
   Michigan 49530, U.S.A. http://www.zondervan.com

Printed in Mexico.

*Building Christian faith in families*

A Lightwave Production
P.O. Box 160 Maple Ridge B.C.,
Canada V2X 7G1

98 99 00 /DR/ 5 4 3 2 1

# Contents

**God Became a Man** ................4-5
   Angels with a Promise

**God's Son Is a Baby** ................6-7
   Rome: The Villages That Ruled
      the World
   Rulers and More Rulers

**28**

**Jesus Grows Up** ........................8-9
   The Jewish World

**Baptized!** ..................................10-11
   Temptation Conquered!
   Jesus Helps Us

**Disciple School** ....................12-13
   Girls Welcome

**24**

**Amazing Miracles** ...............14-15
The Meaning of Miracles

**Teaching with a
Difference** ...........................16-17
Jesus' New Teachings

**Jesus, the Great
Storyteller** ...........................18-19
Great Parables

**Jesus' Last Supper** ................20-21
The "Supper" Today

**15**

**Jesus in the World
Today** .........................................28-29
Changed Lives

**Jesus and
Me** .............30-31

**The Plan Is a
Success!** ..........32

**Jesus' Enemies** ........................22-23
Judas Paid Off
Betrayed!

**Condemned to Death** ........24-25
Why Jesus Had to Die

**The Grave Is Empty!** ............26-27
Risen for Sure!

**32**

# God Became a Man

Did you know Jesus has been alive with God forever?

Imagine an artist becoming part of his own painting! Impossible? God did something like this!

In the very beginning God, through his Son, an awesome artist called the Word, spoke and made the world. "In the beginning, the Word was already there. The Word was with God, and the Word was God. All things were made through him. Nothing that has been made was made without him" (John 1:1, 3). God, through the Word, made every living creature. Then he made people, Adam and Eve, to be like him and be his children. He gave them a beautiful garden to live in and rules to follow so they would have a great life. (A key rule was "Do not eat fruit from the Knowledge tree!") And he gave them free will so they could choose to obey him and be his children. Or not.

Everything should have been fine. But Satan, an important angel who became God's enemy, disguised himself as a snake. "You don't have to obey God's rules," he said. "Eat the Knowledge fruit. You'll become like God."

Unfortunately, Adam and Eve ate it up. They chose to listen to Satan, and that wrecked everything!

God was very sad. He sent Adam and Eve away. He still loved them, but sin separates them from God, who is holy. And everyone who came after them (including us) was born sinful and separated from God, too. God had said, "If you sin, you'll die." So the penalty had to be paid.

Satan thought he'd won. But God had a backup plan! His plan would pay for everyone's sins so we

# Angels with a Promise

God chose human parents for his Son. Mary, and her fiancé, Joseph, from Nazareth. God sent the angel Gabriel to tell Mary, "God is very pleased with you. You will become pregnant and give birth to a son. You must name him Jesus. He will be great and will be called the Son of the Most High God" (Luke 1:30–32). Mary asked how this could happen since she wasn't married. Gabriel said, "The Holy Spirit will come to you. The power of the Most High God will cover you. So the holy one that is born will be called the Son of God" (Luke 1:35).

Joseph found out Mary was pregnant. He knew the baby wasn't his. God sent an angel to Joseph in a dream. He said, "Don't be afraid to take Mary home as your wife. The baby inside her is from the Holy Spirit. She is going to have a son. You must give him the name Jesus. That is because he will save his people from their sins" (Matthew 1:20–21).

So Joseph made Mary his wife.

could all be with him again. God sent his Son, the Word, to die for us. God's Son, Jesus, could pay for our sins because he was holy and sinless. Jesus entered his own "painting" and became one of the people he'd created! "The Word became a human being. He made his home with us…. He came from the Father" (John 1:14). Jesus loved us. He was and is God, the Word. He became human and lived as one of us!

*1) In the beginning there was only God.*

*2) God created the world.*

*3) God made Adam and Eve.*

*4) Adam and Eve disobeyed God and sinned.*

# God's Son Is a Baby

When it was almost time for Mary's baby to be born, the Roman ruler Caesar Augustus made a law that everyone had to go to their hometown to be counted. Joseph belonged to the family line of King David, so he and Mary had to travel from Nazareth up to Bethlehem, the town of David. It must have been a rough journey for Mary.

When they arrived, Bethlehem was so busy that the inn had no room, so Mary and Joseph stayed in a stable. While they were there, Mary gave birth to a baby boy. They called him Jesus, as the angel had said. They wrapped baby Jesus in cloths and made a bed for him in a manger.

That night in the hills near Bethlehem, something amazing happened! An angel of the Lord appeared to shepherds in a field. All around him shone a light. The shepherds were terrified!

The angel told them not to be afraid. He said, "I bring you good news of great joy…. Today in the town of David a Savior has been born to you. He is Christ the Lord. Here is how you will know I am telling you the truth. You will find a baby wrapped in strips of cloth and lying in a manger" (Luke 2:10–12).

The shepherds rushed into Bethlehem and found Mary, Joseph, and baby Jesus. He was wrapped in strips of cloth and lying in a manger just like the angel had said. The shepherds told everyone what had happened. All the people who heard about it were amazed.

God's Son, the Word, was born into our world as the baby Jesus.

# Rome: The Villages That Ruled the World

About 700 years before Jesus was born, a group of villages in Italy joined together to become Rome. This new city was ruled by kings for 200 years. Then it was ruled by two consuls elected each year. One-hundred-fifty years later Rome ruled all of Italy and was conquering other lands with its armies. But the army generals started fighting amongst themselves.

## Rulers and More Rulers

Julius Caesar was elected consul in 59 B.C. He defeated the other generals, unified the empire, and declared himself dictator for life. But the Romans didn't want a dictator and killed him. There were more civil wars until Julius's adopted son, Octavian, won. He restored peace and became Caesar Augustus, the first Roman emperor. He was ruling when Jesus was born.

Whenever the Romans conquered an area, they made the people pay taxes. They stationed very tough soldiers in these new provinces to make sure Roman laws were obeyed and taxes were paid. Their army built excellent roads between major cities and they made Greek the common language throughout the empire.

Rome appointed a man named Herod to be king of Judea where the Jews lived. He ruled over them until a few years after Jesus was born. He built Roman-style cities and tried to introduce Roman customs to the Jews. He built a beautiful temple in Jerusalem for the Jews. This is the temple Jesus visited.

*The Roman Empire covered most of the known world.*

*Roman soldiers wore armor like this.*

# Jesus Grows Up

Have you ever seen a shooting star or comet?

When Jesus was born, Wise Men east of Judea saw an unusual star. They believed it meant a special king had been born to the Jews, so they journeyed to the palace in Jerusalem to look for him. (Where else would a king be?) But the baby wasn't there.

King Herod was upset. He wanted to be the only king. He asked the Jewish leaders where the special King of the Jews would be born. They studied the Scriptures and said, "Bethlehem." The Wise Men found Jesus there with his mother.

They worshiped him and gave him expensive gifts.

That night God warned the Wise Men not to tell Herod about Jesus, so they went home a different way. In a dream, an angel told Joseph to escape to Egypt because Herod wanted to kill Jesus. Joseph got his family up and left right away. The angel was right. Herod killed many babies in Bethlehem hoping the "King of the Jews" would be one of them.

They stayed in Egypt until Herod died. Then, in another dream, an

*Help Mary and Joseph find Jesus*

angel told Joseph it was safe to go home. They returned to live in Nazareth.

Joseph, a carpenter, probably trained Jesus to work with him. They would have made furniture, tools, wheels, and utensils. Jesus likely started school when he was five and learned the Law, Genesis to Deuteronomy in the Bible, and how to read and write.

When Jesus was twelve, he went with his parents to the Passover feast in Jerusalem, to the beautiful temple Herod had built. After the feast, Mary and Joseph left for home. They realized that Jesus wasn't with them and then rushed back to Jerusalem to look for him. After three days, they found him in the temple, sitting with the teachers, listening and asking questions. The people were amazed at him!

Mary said, "Son, why have you treated us like this? Your father and I have been worried about you. We've been looking for you everywhere." "Why were you looking for me?" he asked. "Didn't you know I had to be in my Father's house?" (Luke 2:48–49). Mary and Joseph didn't understand that Jesus was talking about his real Father, God.

Jesus went back to Nazareth with his parents and obeyed them. "Jesus became wiser and stronger. He also became more and more pleasing to God and to people" (Luke 2:52).

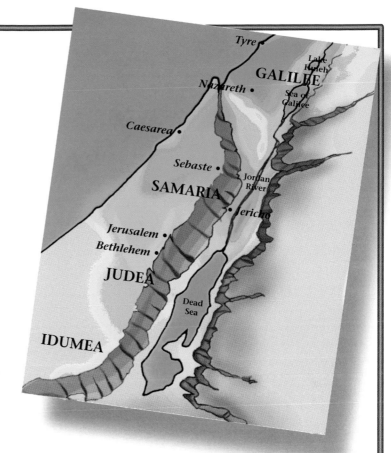

# The Jewish World

Most Jews visited Herod's temple in Jerusalem once or twice a year. The rest of the time they went to the *synagogues* in their own villages to read from the Old Testament and pray.

The Jews had two main political/religious parties. The *Sadducees* were most of the rich. They tried to stay wealthy by cooperating with the Romans. The *Pharisees* were more popular among the common people. They talked about keeping all the rules and details of the Law. The *Sanhedrin* was a Jewish ruling counsel made up of these two groups. They were in charge of everyday life for the Jews.

Many of the Jews hated being ruled by the Romans. They remembered God's promise to send the *Messiah* to *save* the Jews from their enemies. They thought the Messiah would lead an army and defeat the Romans. Jesus didn't come to fight the Romans, so few people believed he was the one they were waiting for.

# Baptized!

Jesus had a cousin named John who was a prophet living in the desert. His message was simple. "Repent [turn back to God] so your sins can be forgiven. The Kingdom of God is near!" When people repented, John baptized them in the Jordan River. Baptism was a symbol of being cleansed from sin.

One day John looked up and saw Jesus in the crowd! He pointed to Jesus and said, "Look! The Lamb of God! He takes away the sin of the world!" (John 1:29). Jesus asked John to baptize him. John protested. After all, Jesus didn't need to repent because he had never sinned! But Jesus said, "'Let it be this way for now. It's right for us to do this. It carries out God's holy plan.' Then John agreed. As soon as Jesus was baptized, he came up out of the water. At that moment heaven was opened. Jesus saw the Spirit of God coming down on him like a dove. A voice from heaven said, 'This is my Son, and I love him. I am very pleased with him'" (Matthew 3:15–17).

Later, Jesus told his followers to be baptized and to baptize others. That's one reason Christians get baptized today. It shows everyone that

God loves us and sent his Son to cleanse us from our sins.

Different churches baptize in different ways. The way it's done is not as important as the reason it's done and what it means: The water is a symbol of Jesus' blood washing away our sins. And baptism represents a commitment of the person's life to God.

# Temptation Conquered!

Satan tricked the first people into disobeying God. Now he tried it with Jesus. He was trying to wreck God's plan. If Jesus gave in to temptation, he wouldn't be able to save the world like God had planned.

After Jesus' baptism, the Holy Spirit led him into the desert. After forty days without food, guess what? He got hungry. Satan told him to make bread out of the stones. He tried to convince Jesus that he deserved to have whatever he wanted. Jesus quoted from the Old Testament and refused.

Satan took Jesus to the top of the temple and told Jesus to jump. This time Satan tried quoting Scripture. He misquoted a psalm, telling Jesus he could do whatever he wanted, even jump off the temple, and nothing bad would happen! Again Jesus refused by quoting the Bible.

Finally, Satan took Jesus to a high mountain and showed him all the powerful kingdoms of the world. He told Jesus he'd give them to him if Jesus worshiped him. Jesus said, "Get away from me, Satan! It's written, 'Worship the Lord your God. He's the only one you should serve'" (Matthew 4:10).

# Jesus Helps Us

We get tempted in similar ways. We want to do things our way instead of God's. Jesus understands what temptation is like. And he knows how we can conquer it. He knew that what God and the Bible said was the truth. So he trusted God and kept his focus on him instead of what he could get for himself. Temptation is Satan's trick to lead us away from the truth. We can fight temptation with the truth of the Bible. We can ask God for help, keep our focus on him, and trust him and Jesus to help us. They will. They love us!

*Jesus knows and understands how we feel.*

# Disciple School

Imagine you're a young Jew in Jesus' time and want to study God's Word. You would look around your neighborhood at the rabbis (teachers). Then you would choose the rabbi you respected, the one you believed really knew the Scriptures.

You would join your *rabbi's* students and sit around him in a classroom. You would listen, ask questions, and memorize what he said until you knew the meaning of the various passages and laws.

However, *understanding* is only part of knowing God's Word. You'd also have to learn how to *live* according to the Torah. So you'd watch your teacher's life carefully. You and the other students or *disciples* would become your rabbi's servants. When your teacher was out and about, you'd walk behind him. You would spend most of your time with him. You'd have a close relationship with him until he decided you were ready to be a teacher yourself. By then you would think, believe, and live like him.

This teaching method was common at that time. Jesus used this teaching method, too. His disciples followed him around, served him, lived with him wherever he went, listened carefully to his teachings, and asked questions. They had a close relationship with Jesus and tried to be like

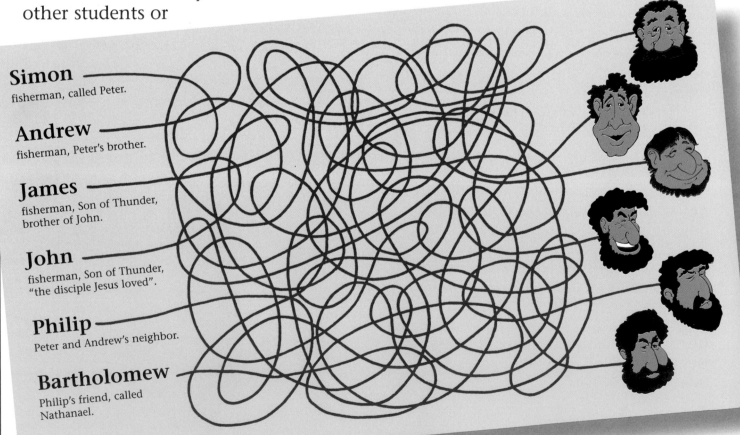

**Simon**
fisherman, called Peter.

**Andrew**
fisherman, Peter's brother.

**James**
fisherman, Son of Thunder, brother of John.

**John**
fisherman, Son of Thunder, "the disciple Jesus loved".

**Philip**
Peter and Andrew's neighbor.

**Bartholomew**
Philip's friend, called Nathanael.

him. But Jesus' disciples didn't choose Jesus as their teacher. Jesus chose them! He chose twelve men. And his disciples didn't learn sitting in a classroom. Jesus taught in public places, on the seashore, in fields, and while they walked around the country.

Jesus chose ordinary men. They were mostly fishermen, but one was a tax collector and one was a "zealot" (someone willing to fight to be free from the Romans). They were people like you and me. Some of them had tempers (Jesus called two of them "Sons of Thunder" because of that), they doubted (remember "Doubting Thomas"?), sometimes they didn't understand, and later on they ran away when Jesus was arrested. But Jesus chose them. And he chooses us.

## Girls Welcome

*"No girls allowed!"* Rabbis didn't teach women. But Jesus did! "The Twelve were with him. So were some women.... These women were helping to support Jesus and the Twelve with their own money" (Luke 8:1, 3).

Some of these women were Mary Magdalene, Joanna, Mary, Salome the mother of the disciples James and John, and Susanna. Jesus had other women friends, like Mary and Martha, the sisters of Lazarus, the man he raised from the dead.

Women were the first to find out Jesus was no longer dead. Women were important to Jesus!

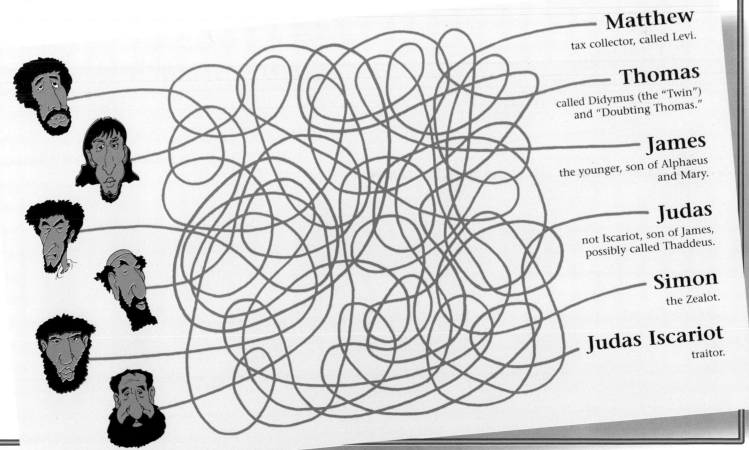

**Matthew**
tax collector, called Levi.

**Thomas**
called Didymus (the "Twin") and "Doubting Thomas."

**James**
the younger, son of Alphaeus and Mary.

**Judas**
not Iscariot, son of James, possibly called Thaddeus.

**Simon**
the Zealot.

**Judas Iscariot**
traitor.

# Amazing Miracles

What's awesome and amazing? A miracle! Better yet, many miracles! Jesus' whole life was full of miracles, from before his birth to after his death and everywhere in between. Jesus experienced miracles and he performed miracles.

## People Miracles

**Jesus healed:** lepers (people with serious skin diseases), at least five blind people, Peter's mother-in-law, a paralyzed man, a man with a withered hand, a woman who'd bled for twelve years, a deaf and dumb man, a woman who'd been bent over for eighteen years, a man who couldn't talk, a man who'd been disabled for thirty-eight years, a man whose ear had been cut off, and, from a distance, one official's sick servant and another's sick son.

**He drove out evil spirits from:** "many," a boy, a man in the synagogue, and at least two violent, super-strong, chain-breaking, tomb-haunting men.

**He raised from the dead:** a twelve-year-old girl, a widow's only son, Lazarus (after he'd been dead four days).

**He fed:** 5000+ people with five loaves of bread and two fish, 4000+ people with seven loaves and a few small fish. The "+" is all the women and children—we don't know how many!

## Nature Miracles

Jesus filled Peter's fishing nets so full they began to break, turned water into wine at a wedding, calmed a storm, walked on water, made a fig tree dry up, and told Peter to go fishing and in the first fish's mouth would be a coin to pay their taxes. After Jesus rose from the dead, he turned the disciples' no-fish night into a too-many-fish-for-the-net night.

*Jesus raised the dead.*

*Jesus walked on water.*

*Jesus fed the hungry.*

*Jesus healed the sick.*

# The Meaning of Miracles

Jesus had a job to do while he was here as a man. A big part of his job was to show people what God was like. Doing miracles was a way to show people that God cared. Jesus showed people God loved them by doing miracles.

Jesus was God. He *told* people what God was like and he *showed* them, by his life and actions. He showed them God cared about little things as well as big ones. (His first miracle was to make water into wine just so his mother's friends wouldn't be embarrassed!)

By healing people, he showed us God is more powerful than sickness and death. He also showed us that God can take care of our needs and then some: Remember the feeding of the 5000+? There was oodles of food left over!

Some saw the miracles and didn't believe, but others did. For example, one night during a storm, the disciples were crossing the lake in their boat. Jesus walked on the water toward them. When he got into the boat, the wind died down. "Then those in the boat worshiped Jesus. They said, 'You really are the Son of God!'" (Matthew 14:33). They *knew* he was God because of the great miracle he had done!

# Teaching with a Difference

Ever had a teacher you loved to listen to, who was interesting and made you think? We can tell from people's responses to Jesus that he was a great teacher. "The crowds were amazed at his teaching. He taught like one who had authority. He didn't speak like their teachers of the law" (Matthew 7:28–29).

These people often heard rabbis and Pharisees teach. But Jesus amazed them! What made him different? He taught as if he "had authority." The rabbis taught what other people said. They didn't teach anything new.

Not Jesus! He'd say things like, "You've heard it said" and quote a famous saying. "Love your neighbor. Hate your enemy." Then he'd add, "But I say" and he'd say something new. "Love your enemies. Pray for those who hurt you" (Matthew 5:43–44). He had authority to add it because he was God.

Jesus also put a new emphasis on old things. He said it's not only important to do the right thing on the outside, we must change on the inside and act from hearts that are right.

The Pharisees believed that to be religious you had to follow all the rules. But Jesus taught that religion isn't about following the rules or obeying detailed commands. It's about a relationship with God. That's why he taught his disciples how to pray so that they could talk to God whenever they wanted, thanking him, and telling him their needs. Prayer helped them get to know God better.

The Pharisees liked to show off how good and generous they were. But Jesus taught us to do good quietly, without expecting

*Jesus walked everywhere, probably in sandals like these.*

anything in return. He showed that a widow who gave only two pennies was more generous in her heart than a rich person who gave a big gift from great wealth.

Jesus' teaching was almost the opposite of the Pharisees' teaching. No wonder he got people's attention!

# Jesus' New Teachings

**Be Born Again:**

"No one can see God's kingdom without being born again. No one can enter God's kingdom without being born through water and the Holy Spirit. People give birth to people. But the Spirit gives birth to spirit. God loved the world so much that he gave his one and only Son. Anyone who believes in him will not die but will have eternal life" (John 3:3, 5–6, 16).

**The Lord's Prayer:**

"This is how you should pray. 'Our Father in heaven, may your name be honored. May your kingdom come. May what you want to happen be done on earth as it's done in heaven. Give us today our daily bread. Forgive us our sins, just as we also have forgiven those who sin against us. Keep us from falling into sin when we're tempted. Save us from the evil one'" (Matthew 6:9–13).

*Jesus taught wherever he went.*

# Jesus, the Great Storyteller

"Once upon a time." These words mean a story is coming. Everyone likes stories! Jesus knew that, and told a lot of them. But many of his started with, "The kingdom of God is like." Then he'd launch into a story or parable that compared something people knew, like seeds or sheep, to things they didn't know, like God's kingdom. The comparisons helped them understand the kingdom. For example, Jesus spent time with people like tax collectors that the Jews looked down on and called "sinners." They thought God wanted them to avoid sinners. So Jesus told a story to help them understand that God wants to save sinners—"lost" people.

He said, "Suppose one of you has 100 sheep and loses one of them. Won't he leave the 99 in the open country? Won't he go and look for the one lost sheep until he finds it? When he finds it, he'll joyfully put it on his shoulders and go home. Then he'll call his friends and neighbors together. He'll say, 'Be joyful with me. I've found my lost sheep.' I tell you, it'll be the same in heaven. There'll be great joy when one sinner turns away from sin. Yes, there'll be more joy than for 99 godly people who don't need to turn away from their sins" (Luke 15:3–7).

His disciples asked why he used parables. He told them they had been given the chance to understand the secrets of God's kingdom. Jesus meant that those who wanted to understand his stories and teaching would. Those who didn't, would just hear a story.

## Great Parables

**The Prodigal Son Parable** teaches that God is the best father we can imagine! A son left home and did wrong, foolish things. He spent everything he had and was starving. Finally, he decided to go home and ask for forgiveness. The father was so happy that he threw a party for him! Our Father, God, is like that (Luke 15:11–32).

**The Good Samaritan Parable** teaches that our neighbor is anyone in need. A Jewish man was beaten by robbers and left for dead. Jewish leaders walked by without helping. A Samaritan (Jews disliked Samaritans) stopped to help. Who acted like a good neighbor? (Luke 10:25–37)

**The Sower and Seeds** teaches us that people respond to Jesus in different ways. A farmer plants in different kinds of soil. Some seeds don't grow, some get choked by weeds, some have shallow roots and wither, and some grow and give a good crop (Matthew 13:1–23).

**The Weeds Parable** tells us we can't always tell who belongs to God's kingdom and who doesn't. An enemy sowed bad seed in a field. The owner said to let the weeds grow with the wheat. They'd sort it out at harvest. We shouldn't judge people. Instead, we should let God sort out who belongs to him (Matthew 13:24–30).

**The Parable of the House Built on Rock** teaches that when we live God's way things work out for the best. Jesus said people who heard his words and lived by them were wise like a house-builder who built on rock. But foolish people were like those who built on sand. A storm came and CRASH! No more sand-house (Matthew 7:24–27).

# Jesus' Last Supper

Long ago, about 1500 years before Jesus, the Jews (Israelites) were slaves in Egypt. The Egyptian king, Pharaoh, was stubborn. He didn't want to set them free. God sent plagues to show the Egyptians he was more powerful than their so-called "gods." In the last plague, every first-born child in the land would die.

Moses, the Israelite leader, told his people to kill a lamb and put some of its blood on the top and sides of their doors. God said he would see it and pass over (skip) any house with blood on the door. The lamb died in place of the eldest child. Meanwhile, the Israelites ate their lamb dinner with unleavened (flat) bread and wine. This was the first "Passover." That night the first-born children of all the Egyptians died, but the Israelite children were safe. Pharaoh let the Israelites go. Jews celebrate the Passover every year as a reminder of their escape.

Jesus celebrated the Passover with his disciples. This time it would be different!

After the meal, Jesus took the unleavened bread. "He gave thanks and broke it. He handed it to them and said, 'This is my body. It's given for you. Every time you eat it, do it in memory of me.'" After supper he took the wine. "'This cup is the new covenant [agreement] in my blood. It's poured out to forgive the sins of many'" (Luke 22:19–20; Matthew

26:28). Jesus was about to become the Passover lamb. He would die instead of everyone who had sinned.

# The "Supper" Today

When Adam and Eve sinned God said the punishment was death. Later he made a covenant with the Israelites. They would regularly bring sacrifices to pay for their sins. Animals would die in their place, and God would forgive them.

Now, in Jesus, God was about to make a new covenant with all people. In this new agreement, there's no need for regular sacrifices. Only one is needed. God would provide it himself: his sinless Son, Jesus. When Jesus told the disciples to eat the bread and drink the cup, he was telling them to accept what he was about to do for them.

Jesus' last supper with his disciples started a new tradition that we still celebrate almost 2000 years later! People have

different names for it, but when we eat the bread and drink from the cup, we're all saying, "I accept what Jesus did for me. I know he paid for my sins so that I wouldn't have to die. Thank you!"

# Jesus' Enemies

Jesus preached the truth, told people about God's kingdom, and showed them God's love. But he still had enemies. The Pharisees, Sadducees, chief priests, and scribes all hated Jesus. They loved to be respected and to have power and authority. They were afraid Jesus would change that.

The Pharisees liked to impress people. They felt it was their job to keep all Jews obeying the Law. They made lots of new laws. They were sure they were God's favorites!

Along came Jesus telling everyone the Pharisees weren't as wonderful as they thought: The Pharisees had it wrong. God wanted people to obey him from love, not fear; to treat people with kindness, not to be proud and judgmental. The Sanhedrin with its Pharisees, Sadducees, and priests, knew that if people listened to Jesus instead of them, they'd lose their power. Or the Romans might get upset and take their power away.

They decided it was time to do something about Jesus! Since only the Romans could put people to death, the Jews had to convince Pilate, the Roman governor, that Jesus was against Caesar and deserved to die.

They knew that if they arrested Jesus when he was surrounded by the people there would be a riot. If only they could get him alone.

## Judas Paid Off

"Traitor." "Tattle-tale." "Judas." We all know these words. But why do we use "Judas" to mean someone who betrays a friend? Because of Judas Iscariot, Jesus' disciple.

Judas snuck off to see the Pharisees. "Hey!" he said. "You want Jesus? I can give you Jesus. But it'll cost you." So the Pharisees gave Judas thirty pieces of silver (about five months' pay)

22

to tell them where they could quietly capture Jesus.

Jesus and the disciples were in the Garden of Gethsemane. Peter told Jesus, "I'll give my life for you." Jesus answered, "Will you really? Before the rooster crows, you'll say three times that you don't know me!" (John 13:38) Later, the disciples slept while Jesus prayed, "My Father, if it's possible, take this cup of suffering away from me. But let what you want be done, not what I want" (Matthew 26:39).

# Betrayed!

Suddenly soldiers, officials, and a crowd with swords and clubs (sent from the Jewish leaders) arrived in the quiet Garden. Judas was leading them! He betrayed Jesus. When Jesus was arrested, the disciples ran away.

*The Garden of Gethsemane where Jesus prayed.*

Jesus was taken to the high priest's house. The Sanhedrin was there even though they weren't supposed to meet at night. They took him to Pilate, the Roman governor, saying that Jesus called himself "King of the Jews" and was against Caesar.

Peter had followed the crowd into the courtyard. Someone asked if he was Jesus' disciple. He said, "No!" This happened twice more. The third time Peter was so scared he swore and said, "I don't know this man you're talking about!" (Mark 14:71). Right away the rooster crowed. Peter remembered what Jesus had said. He ran out, crying.

Jesus was passed from the Jews to Pilate, to Herod, and back to Pilate. Pilate found Jesus innocent but, trying to please the Jews, had him beaten anyway. The Jews told Pilate he wasn't Caesar's friend if he let Jesus go. Pilate got scared and agreed to crucify Jesus.

*Coins from Jesus' time.*

# Condemned to Death

Crucifixion was a horrible way to die. Roman solders were known for their cruelty. Jesus had already been beaten, mocked, spit on, whipped, and had a "crown" made of thorns pushed onto his head. Now he had to carry part of his own cross outside the city to the place called "Skull," "Golgotha," or "Calvary."

Jesus' hands and feet were nailed to the cross. Two robbers were crucified with him, one on each side. On the top of Jesus' cross Pilate put a sign: "This is the King of the Jews." One of the robbers believed this. He asked Jesus to remember him when he came into his kingdom. Jesus answered, "Today you'll be with me in paradise" (Luke 23:43). Then, speaking about those who had put him on the cross, Jesus said, "Father, forgive them. They don't know what they're doing" (Luke 23:34).

Many strange things happened. At noon "the whole land was covered with darkness until three o'clock. The sun had stopped shining. Jesus cried out, 'My God, my God, why have you deserted me?' The temple curtain was torn in two. The earth shook. Tombs broke open. The bodies of many who had died were raised to life. Jesus called out in a loud voice, 'Father, into your hands I commit my very life.' After he said this, he took his last breath. He said, 'It is finished.' Then he bowed his head and died. The Roman commander and those guarding Jesus saw the earthquake and all that had happened. They were terrified. They exclaimed, 'He was surely the Son of God!'"

(Matthew 27:46, 51–52, 54; Luke 23:44–46; John 19:30).

Satan used people to kill Jesus. He thought he'd won. He didn't know it was all part of God's plan. Friends of Jesus took his body down, wrapped it in burial cloths with some spices, and laid it in a tomb nearby.

Jesus had said he would rise again after three days. His enemies remembered. They asked Pilate to station Roman soldiers in front of Jesus' tomb in case his disciples tried to steal his body and pretend he'd risen from the dead.

# Why Jesus Had to Die

God's plan was almost complete! Since Adam and Eve had sinned, God had been working to make a way for us to have the close relationship with him he'd wanted from the beginning. Sin separated us from God. The only way we could be forgiven once and for all was if someone sinless chose to pay for our sins and die in our place. Only God was sinless. So God chose to die for us.

God's Son, Jesus Christ, the Word who had made everything, became flesh like us and lived a perfect, sinless life. Then Jesus fulfilled God's plan and died a horrible death.

He died at Passover. He was the Passover lamb, the one who died instead of us, just like the lamb in the first Passover died in place of the first-born child. Now Jesus' blood paid for our sins. The Bible says, "Without the spilling of blood, no one can be forgiven" (Hebrews 9:22). And "Because of what the Son has done, we have been set free. Because of him, all of our sins have been forgiven" (Colossians 1:14).

What a plan! What love!

# The Grave Is Empty!

The Roman soldiers stood guard over Jesus' tomb from Friday evening to Sunday morning. YAWN! Suddenly the earth shook. An angel rolled the stone away from the tomb! The Romans "were so afraid of him that they shook and became like dead men" (Matthew 28:4).

Some of Jesus' women followers came to the tomb. The angel said, "Don't be afraid. I know that you're looking for Jesus, who was crucified. He isn't here! He's risen, just as he said he would! Come and see the place where he was lying. Go quickly! Tell his disciples, 'He has risen from the dead'" (Matthew 28:5–7). They ran to tell the news!

Peter and John ran to the tomb and found it empty. Later, the disciples were in a room and Jesus appeared! He spoke to them and ate with them. Jesus appeared many times over the next forty days and explained the Scriptures.

After forty days, Jesus led his disciples to the Mount of Olives. "Then he lifted up his hands and blessed them. While he was blessing them, he left them. He was taken up into heaven. They watched until a cloud hid him from their sight. They kept on looking at the sky. Suddenly two men dressed in white clothing stood beside them. 'Men of Galilee,' they said, 'why do you stand here looking at the sky? Jesus has been taken away from you into heaven. But he'll come back in the same way you saw him go'" (Luke 24:50–51; Acts 1:9–11). Only God could have done that!

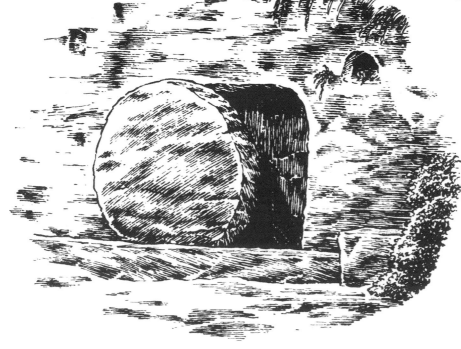

*The huge stone was rolled away from Jesus' tomb.*

# Risen for Sure!

Was the resurrection real? Put these facts together.

- The Romans said Jesus was dead. People do not recover from crucifixion.

- Jesus was buried in a cave with one exit.

- His body was wrapped in cloths and spices. The myrrh used made the grave-clothes stick to the body so they'd be difficult to remove.

- A large stone (probably almost two tons) was rolled across the entrance.

- Roman soldiers guarded the tomb. Falling asleep on the job meant death for them!

A couple of days later:

- The tomb was empty.

- The huge stone had been moved away from the tomb.

- The Roman guards were bribed to say the disciples stole the body while they slept. But neither they nor the disciples were punished for breaking Roman law.

- The grave-clothes were empty, as if his body had passed right through them.

- More than 500 people said Jesus appeared to them alive!

- The disciples changed from timid people hiding from the authorities, to bold people who suffered beatings and death because they believed Jesus rose from the dead.

The only story that fits the facts is that Jesus really did rise from the dead, just as Scripture and Jesus predicted!

*Adapted from Josh McDowell's book* Reasons Skeptics Should Consider Christianity.

# Jesus in the World Today

Look for Israel on a world map. It's a tiny place by the Mediterranean Sea. What could such a small place have to offer the world? Only the greatest man who ever lived!

In some ways, Jesus' life doesn't seem unusual. (Let's ignore the miracles for a bit.) He was born in a tiny village. After his trip to Egypt, he never traveled more than 150 miles from home and all of that on foot. He was a carpenter until he was about thirty. Then he was a traveling preacher for three years with no home, very little money, and only the clothes on his back. He hung out with people others looked down on.

Then people turned against him, his friends ran away, and one of them betrayed him. He was condemned to death and nailed to a cross. As he died Roman soldiers gambled over his clothes. His body was put in a borrowed grave.

Jesus lived and died in obedience to God. And then something incredible happened. Jesus rose from the dead and changed things forever! In the almost 2000 years since then, this man from a tiny corner of the world has had a greater impact than anyone else who ever lived!

Jesus' followers wrote books and letters about his life and teachings that are among the most-read books in the world. Whole libraries have been written about Jesus and his teachings. Easter and Christmas are celebrated. Jesus' followers around the world number in the millions. His churches are in every major city, and in towns and villages throughout the world. Jesus' story has been translated into hundreds of languages so people everywhere can know him. Colleges, universities, and even nations have been started based on his teachings.

Jesus' life changed the world forever! That was God's plan.

# Changed Lives

Have you ever tried to break a habit, like biting your fingernails? Changing is hard! Just think, then, how hard it is to change from a frightened person into a brave one! That's what happened to Jesus' disciples almost overnight! How? Because Jesus rose from the dead. That showed the disciples he really was the Messiah they'd been looking for. It gave them courage to stand up for the truth.

After Jesus died, the disciples hid in the upper room with the door locked. They were afraid the Jews would kill them next. That's where Jesus found them and showed them he was alive again. When he rose to heaven he promised them that a friend, a Comforter, would help them. When the Comforter, the Holy Spirit, came, they changed completely (see Acts 2). Instead of hiding, they boldly told people about Jesus. They were threatened, arrested, and beaten, but they didn't stop! They were no longer afraid of people who could only kill their bodies. If Jesus rose from the dead, they would too. Their changed lives showed they knew Jesus was alive. (Would you die for something you knew was a lie?)

Jesus has been changing lives ever since. And he can change your life too. Just ask him. It's as easy as that!

# Jesus and Me

**Q Why does Jesus want us to follow him?**

**A** Jesus told the people to follow him because he is the way to God, heaven, and eternal life. When Jesus was on earth, the disciples and others followed him by walking close

to him and listening to his words. Today, we follow Jesus by copying his example and by doing what he says. We can find out what he says by reading the Bible.

**Key Verses:** "Then Jesus spoke to his disciples. 'If you want to follow me,' he said, 'you must say no to yourself. You must take your cross and follow me. If you want to save your life, you will lose it. But if you lose your life for me, you will find it. What good is it for you to gain the whole world but lose your soul? Or what can you trade for your soul?'" (Matthew 16:24–26)

**Q How do you get Jesus in your heart?**

**A** You become a Christian by asking Jesus to take over your life. You know that you have done wrong things, that you have sinned, and you recognize that you need Jesus to forgive

your sins. So you tell Jesus about your sins and that you are sorry, and you ask for his forgiveness. Then you do what Jesus says.

**Key Verses:** "But now God has shown us how to become right with him. The Law and the Prophets give witness to this. It has nothing to do with obeying the law. We are made right with God by putting our faith in Jesus Christ. That happens to all who believe. It is no different for the Jews than for anyone else. Everyone has sinned. No one measures up to God's glory. The free gift of God's grace makes all of us right with him. Christ Jesus paid the price to set us free" (Romans 3:21–24).

## Q How can Jesus fit in my heart?

A When we say "heart," we mean deep down inside us where we really feel and believe. So when someone says, "Jesus lives in my heart," the person means that he has asked Jesus to be his Savior to forgive and take care of him

and that Jesus is in charge of his life. When someone asks Jesus to take over, God really does come inside. The Holy Spirit comes and lives inside that person. And the Holy Spirit can be in all of the people who love God at the same time. Jesus wants to be very close to you, too, like a good friend. Through the Holy Spirit, he wants to "live in your heart."

**Key Verses:** "That word contains the mystery that has been hidden for many ages. But now it has been made known to God's people. God has chosen to make known to them the glorious riches of that mystery. He has made it known among those who aren't Jews. And here is what it is. Christ is in you. He is your hope of glory" (Colossians 1:26–27).

## Q When is Jesus coming back?

A Before Jesus left the earth many years ago, he promised to return some day. And after Jesus went up into the clouds, angels said he would come back eventually. No one knows exactly when that will happen. It could be any day now. For Christians, this is a wonderful event to look forward to. Christ's return will be the beginning of the end for Satan and all evil in the world. Won't it be great to see Jesus in person! Although no one knows when Christ will return, he told us to be ready. This means living the way he would want us to, using our time wisely, and telling others about God's Good News.

**Key Verses:** "[Jesus is speaking] No one knows about that day or hour. Not even the angels in heaven know. The Son does not know. Only the Father knows. So keep watch. You do not know on what day your Lord will come" (Matthew 24:36, 42).

*from* 101 Questions Children Ask About God, *Livingstone Corporation and Lightwave Publishing, 1992.*

# The Plan Is a Success!

God's plan worked! Ever since Adam and Eve sinned, God was working to make a way for people (that's us) to have the kind of relationship with him he wanted. He knew we would only really be happy if we were close to him. But sin made a wall between us. God needed someone to break down the wall. He needed a perfect person, someone without sin, who would be willing to die to pay for our sin.

So God got everything ready and made sure the timing was perfect. Then he sent his Son, the Word, through whom he created everything, to be born as a baby and live as a human. He called him "Jesus," which means "Savior."

Jesus grew up as an ordinary person. He lived a perfect, obedient life. He never sinned. Like us, he faced temptations and had struggles. He grew and learned. The Bible tells us "Jesus was God's Son. But by suffering he learned what it means to obey" (Hebrews 5:8). He died for us, to pay for our sins. And he broke down the wall sin had made between us and God. God accepted Jesus' death in place of ours and forgave us our sins!

That was God's plan. That's why Jesus came: to show us what God was like, to teach us how to relate to God, and to pay for our sins so that we could be together with God as God had planned even before he made us.

All we have to do is accept what Jesus did, ask for forgiveness, and, with God's help, try to live the way he wants us to.

Then we wait for Jesus to come back and take us to heaven with him. That's where we'll be with God fully and be completely happy!